"In her terrific new book *Seeing Things*, Marjorie Maddox affirms the charities of attention as key to understanding, if not ameliorating, problems of fracture, disintegration, depression, disease. To 'see things' is to hallucinate, but never that alone. In poems of keen observation and formal beauty, the thingness of the imaginal acquires the stubborn presence of the undeniable, tangible, real. It articulates the crisis of a divided sensibility with a cry, a call to see through "the bright glare of what we hide/ from each other," to affirm, with unsentimental precision of heart and mind, the prospect of a more inclusive gaze. What could be more timely in an age dominated by image, appearance, lies? 'Where shall we hide from the pain that bore us,' the author asks, 'from the damaged selves that keep us dying?' Nowhere and everywhere. the poems suggest. In line after line, imagination binds us, makes a sacrament of heartbreak, lifts the veil on a spiritual infusion, the ghost that inhabits the body of world. Marjorie Maddox offers, in valorization of the shared, something of the truly exceptional: a visionary book."
—Bruce Bond, author of *Vault*

"*Seeing Things* tells one story of a family under stress and navigating with grace to heal. It is a page-turner that all of us can read with fascination because in many ways, it is our story too. It's surely one of the best books I have read this year."
—Jeanne Murray Walker, author of *Leaping from the Burning Train*

"Marjorie Maddox's aptly titled *Seeing Things* pulls us in precise lines to witness the daily struggles of the world we often turn away from—disease, mental illness, the devastating slow disappearance of a mother and her memory. Utilizing a variety of forms, Maddox traverses rooms of sorrow, and rooms of singing, and in the end offers us, in the face of grief, a profound love of life 'claiming praise as respite, holding close each breaking day.'"
—Sean Thomas Dougherty, author of *Death Prefers the Minor Keys*

"In *Seeing Things*, Maddox reminds us that the mind and body often choose our meditations and fates independent of our wills. In middle age, her speaker watches her daughter, the woman she has nurtured to adulthood, and her mother, the woman that nurtured her, reel with disillusion and disability, unstable like our wounded planet subjected to random violence and ecological

catastrophe. Hers is the voice of maturity caring for her own old wounds in the midst of many uncertainties, her poems admitting that she is sometimes not seeing well or still learning how to see, and admonishing us to question our perceptions also. *Seeing Things* is sagacious and relatable. We need more wisdom in this world. We need poets like Maddox helping us to see."
—Kimberly Ann Priest, author of *Slaughter the One Bird*

"'Just like that,' the poet writes, 'the invisible shifts to visible.' However, in this remarkable book, Marjorie Maddox shows us that, yes, we are 'seeing things' physically, psychologically, artistically, imaginatively, and spiritually—and that yes, we are perceiving clearly, but only when we see through the lens of love and hope. Though we are often 'wounded and weeping,' the poet writes, we must 'Open the window and sing!' Ultimately, she says, 'Step out / with arms open, and eyes gathering / vim and vision: grandeur...'"
—Lois Roma-Deeley, Poet Laureate of Scottsdale, AZ, and author of *Like Water in the Palm of My Hand*

"'We claim one life rewrites the rest,' but how should we begin? Marjorie Maddox shows us how in this beautifully wrought collection. Among these poems are explorations of aging, mothers and daughters, caring for family members with dementia, trauma, and 'days holy and unholy.' You'll also find gurgling hope, a small gray rabbit, the apple scent of hair in October, and a working radio still playing the oldies. There is a carefully constructed intimacy in these poems shaped by a firm resolve in the 'layered song of sentences' inviting you to embark on a worthy voyage and better understand that 'perhaps it's snow that filters out the light, perhaps it's dusk.'"
—Connie Post, author of *Between Twilight* and *Broken Metronome*

Seeing
Things

Marjorie Maddox

Wildhouse
Poetry

Design by Melody Stanford Martin

Front Cover image: *Your Move*, Anna Lee Hafer

Published by Wildhouse Poetry, an imprint of Wildhouse
Publishing (www.wildhousepublishing.com). No part of this
book may be reproduced in any manner without written
permission from the publisher, except in brief quotations
embodied in critical articles or reviews. Contact info@
wildhousepublications.com for all requests.

Printed in the USA

ISBN 978-1-961741-19-5

*To my daughter
and in memory of my mother,
strong women both*

Contents

III. Holding Close Each Breaking Day

I

Between the Mind's Two Worlds

Guardian

I wanted them to be angels—the people
my daughter saw, the ones not
really there—angels without webbed wings
but ethereal still in the midnight outside air
where she stood, head cocked, painting the world's
darkness. Angel, I wanted you to be. The people
my daughter saw, the ones not
you in the paint-thick air in your
ethereal midnight—did you see them, too,
their heads cocked, watching my daughter's
darkness. Guardian, O guardian, with your seraphim-
borrowed slippers, you tiptoe along the corpus callosum
between the mind's two worlds:
this one at the end of the driveway
where the men clothed in shadows
hide in midnight's peripheral,
and this one, where we wear the unseen's
shadows, where your celestia limbs
flap back fear, where my daughter
keeps painting her inside midnight
as she cocks her head just so before turning
sharply to your entering or leaving.

Seeing Things

Just like that the invisible shifts to visible,
reality's bold finger of light
taps something here in the mind, dimmed
fear suddenly spotlighted, its name
elusive but its image clear-faced and whole
like the hallucinations once hidden

in my daughter's brain, no longer hidden.
Outside our house, a father, invisible
to others, walks towards her. And yet, the whole
night he sleeps beside me. Morning's light
does nothing with such visions but name
them "crazy," less than whole,

and yet all around me—dimmed
in the reality of every day—the hidden
angels and saints somehow still name
the invisible within the visible,
still break the shadows with light.
And can this make us whole?

When Merton spoke of such whole-
ness, did he know the mystery of our dim
lives that still serve as light
to others' visions, too often hidden
beneath a thousand bushels, until, visible
again, they shine a common name?

Today, the world's chaos speaks name-
lessness but not meekly, no holy
call to seek fecundity in the invisible.
Instead, the ancient revelations dim
beside the bright glare of what we hide
from each other. Take the truer light
of what binds these worlds and lightens
our heavy but shared epiphanies—boldly named

or meekly nameless, spirits hidden
and revealed, our hope for whole-
ness. Come, though our visions dim,
we trudge and trip together towards such light

where . . . *in all visible things an invisible*
fecundity, a dimmed light, a meek name-
lessness, a hidden wholeness.

Ode to Daughter as Artist

Praise for the spontaneous
paint splatter; for the blank
wide face of canvas; the thin

stroke of clear; the unannounced
swirl and burst of emergence:
oils and newsprint surging

into bright, wild collage,
hue and creativity tottering
on eternity, one-day only. Or not,

the heft of 3-D spinning now
into something unlike
anything, like steady

chalk or premeditated
ink. No. Rather
thought and arm high

on epiphany,
and the brilliant eye
that arrives there

in an ordinary room,
on an ordinary day: art &
its dizzying versions of birth.

After the diagnosis,

the doctor who dismissed her
complaints now calls every morning,

brings Cookie Dough ice cream
to the hospital, on his lunch break

arrives with cheeseburger and fries
bathed in grease and gossip

about his other "loser" patients, the not-
pretty ones who don't garner such attention.

With a boyish smile, he tosses out
quick comments to coax

her skeleton body to eat, regain
lost confidence and weight,

her blood cell count swimming
swiftly towards death and lawsuit.

Though we demand an end
to such solicitations, the phone

keeps ringing, his shaky voice,
she tells us, both arrogant

and scared, asking far away
on the other end, "And how

are we today? And how
is our favorite patient?"

Ode to Almost-Silence

Praise to the door clicking shut,
to absence warming up the room,

but not completely: fireplace flame still
spitting its lazy opinions, radiator

humming its calm, the floorboard's creak
letting you know it's still there

but won't interrupt like the brash
morning jazz your husband plays

before coffee opens the ears
to thought and conversation.

Here: the louder hush of outside world
kept out—wind, occasional cat,

an emergency (not yours)
begging for someone else

to run, or fix, or bark commands
that can't break into this cordoned-off

zone of chosen contemplation—
where sometimes, even now, you hear

the memory of waves, the scratch
of sole on sand, the swirl of shells, and even

your chin lifting into salty air
as you listen not for the lost

and gone but for what is
there and here inside

the ear and the empty
house, not empty after all.

8

The artist at the colony asks me if I'm famous,

if I'm someone she should know,
pay attention to, bother having coffee with,
talk with about the father who raped her at twelve,
about my father, about the slant of rainy light after
you're weeping for half a life and then some and
when/if you leave the toilet paper unwinding from the top
or bottom, and what our papas said the two days after,
and avocados and kumquats, and the strange
geometric shapes that cascade into our dreams
five days each year before the equinox, and if
I'm well known enough for her to pry open my palm
and slice my life lines with an X-Acto knife—would I
do that for her?—and have I won a Pulitzer yet, and
what color were the eyes of God when I looked straight
at him for three minutes without blinking once, Ok
maybe once, and may she have that last bottle of wine,
could she borrow a g ass, and how much does *The New Yorker*
pay, do I think they would consider her work, she's started
writing, too, have I slept with anyone there, and does the mold
in my studio make my eyes itch in the morning—or evening,
she's heard both—because she really wants to know about the time
the London editor who knew the New York editor who knew me
from someone at the colony or raved about my work on Eskimos or
transplants or something like that and later sat on a committee
that judged that really important prize—she can't remember
which one right now because, thanks again, she had a bit too much
of my Merlot, but am I that writer, the one she's heard
something about, the one she should know?
No, I say, no, though I am someone
writing, trying to write, someone.

Bipolar Triolet

— to A. L.

No one understands.
Insight, foresight, hindsight:
Darkness oozes;
no one understands to help.
paralyzing lethargy,
such labyrinthine reality
to No. To help me,
within my non-sight or,

Help me to see.
all sight gone.
only wounds are real:
See me:
all-consuming energy,
that belongs
understand alone. See
in hindsight, I'll be gone.

Suicide Drafts

When my childhood friend calls, I am writing the pain of my daughter.
It is the same sound as her daughter's siren, now cracking the ordinary air.
If her daughter recovers, mine will as well. To even utter that other

life. . .? On the phone, we can't speak what could be. Mothers
mother each other—or else our already swollen fear
when our child calls would write this pain too real. Daughter

of my friend, your siren sounds our distance, speaks the terror
I swallow each day. Friend, when is *I'm here* enough to cut despair
from *if*. . . ? My daughter recovers. Yours will as well. Let's utter lies to each other

until they're true. Today's skies collapse: no words to say *I love her*
enough in this weather of ordinary lives bone-bare
when childhood writes its pain. My friend calls. I write my daughter

to remind her of sky, of the sharp turns of weather, that I love her
laughter and the apple scent of her hair in October, that where
if utters her *well*, we will recover. Daughter of mine, I can't even *if* the other

aloud in this autumn air traveling fast towards other mothers
who dare not stare into the evening, not knowing whether/
when a childhood friend will call. I am the pain writing my daughter
into my friend's daughter, recovery ours. We utter it now for each other.

Photo with Bald Heads

— for Anya Krugovoy Silver and Noah Silver

Or nearly; the baby fuzz is hers,
compliments of the cancer we seldom speak,

though she does—loudly and often—but not now.
Instead, on this matte finish, she calmly cradles

the red-faced infant, his small mouth open,
life from the still-living pulsing.

His soft spot already
sprouts strands she'll touch

and touch again. See
how she stares out at us

or at God, just this side of the picture-
perfect smile she owns

in the bright flash
of her dark room. See how

she embraces, with her
sleep-deprived, wide-

awake eyes, much more
than the omniscient

one-eyed camera
could ever claim. Only she

can reveal her *See*
this is me there, here, now,

grabbing my own ever after,
the camera clicks and subtle shifts

that follow: her liturgy not of beginnings
or ends, but persistence, holy continuation

into our space of now, brimming
just so with this immortal moment of joy.

Ode to Son as Encyclopedia

Praise the sage arrangement
of dates first in the hippocampus,
then the cerebral cortex efficiently
paired with the best
available synapse 3000 BCE, AD 29,
                375, 1338, 1492,
                1665, 1776
each year stacked, pattern
the poster child of memory,
which—digits neat in their slots—
you can't help coveting
1863, 1914, 1939,
1953, 1963, 1980,
1991, 2001
nations' births
and destructions
prioritized—all this
at your ready access except
your latest interaction with socks
or grocery list, which somehow
slip past the brain's rolodex
or encyclopedic entries. Blessed
though be 1999,
                and the sequence
                of your days,
                each minute its own
                repeated blessing
                in the Year of Our Lord.
                Amen.

Prayer for Three Women, Twenty-One and Under

3:00 a.m. and, again, I wake saying your names.
Even the streetlights are out, shattered by somebody's stones,
and dark shapes itself only around some stray dog barking.
Of course, the world is cold, no warmth from my words,
and yet I pray them anyway, hold on to the vowels of your sighs.

Where are you sleeping now, no-daughter-of-mine but one I loved
for your love of someone I love, your whole-body smile towards him?
In the distance, your long hair hovers above your retreating shadow.

And what are you dreaming now, daughter of my friend,
floating away from the room where you've locked yourself
to protect yourself? The trees sing your silhouette
until you answer with stars,
dark and deep.

And what are you praying now, daughter-of-mine
who does not pray but draws the leaving, the singing, the locking,
the stars lodged deep in my own dark throat, reciting all your names,

ones I, too, claimed in the escaping, in the letting go,
in the fear that shatters words and then remakes them at 3:00 a.m.,
returning sighs to this night—where fear still hovers over the found
and floundering, listening for names—yours and mine—
in the harsh bark of strays, in the fierce petitions of the lost.

Auto-, Bio-, Graphy

I have written you before,
thirty years and the burned

still smolder on air,
singed confetti that knows no

celebration but this:
You were once the sky,

not torn letters disguised as embers,
not disintegrating ash.

Your voice crackled across night,
covered everything. This is

the memory of the forgotten,
the sight of the color-blind

when smoky fog swirls, lifts, descends,
rises and falls again, syllables somewhere

undetected but known
the way one slight motion can alter

temperature, shape, decades—
and suddenly nothing that was

is or is consistently inside the eye
that read your undoing closely.

Even you are more than one,
are her or them sorting the tattered

that once held my name, a speck
of incombustible ink, invisible

temporarily (yes, perhaps),
but in this climate, permanent

after all, each fleck of word,
each story backlighting the moon

that shifted just enough now
to rewrite the sun.

On a Hot Summer Night for Revenge

At thirteen, you scream, "Get your hands off me!"
so loudly that the pale-blue venetian blinds

of your half-opened bedroom window rattle
the way—clear across your dusty room

with its piles of dirty clothes—my breath catches
with a click-swish of time and raised fists,

real ones that did their own scheming,
not your hot-night calculations to escape chores. Still,

by habit, I back into the corner beside your cluttered desk
where you imagine letters from the man you didn't know,

who left his signature on my chest when I didn't scream,
"Get your hands off me!" out an opened window,

or maybe when I did, but no dutiful neighbor called
for the police or the ambulance that I now imagine

skidding, twelve years tardy, around the corner of here
and now, lights spinning emergency, sirens blaring help.

Maybe now they'll come, the uniformed protection, pounding
on the door, heeding the new neighbors' false suspicions,

promising to take me away—or you—who do not yet know
how pain blooms in heat, how truth sacrifices its shirt

to cover scars much deeper than this argument
over independence and unmade beds, which you

may or may not remember on some other blistering night
when we sip ice tea, laugh, and flick on the TV

to watch the latest family drama while, in the distant
background, neighborhood sirens continue to scream.

Trust,

so easy to unlearn, easier still to forget
the faces of those who earned it fair-and-square
before something—a light switch, a sound—
replace the just-opened eyes, the silent ear,
even the slight blush of cheeks with something
akin to ominous. Recoil and run
is the way to go when fear's tattooed
the inside of the brain, synapse after synapse
signaling S.O.S to the next and next and next generations
even when the path is clear and the flow of truth
steady. Yes, everyday veins can handle
the heavy, but let's switch stories. Do you
remember your narrative when I ran—
what was left of my heart heaving—
into you? Can I remember your tightrope
of certainty disintegrating? Even
the indelibly inked veins can be removed,
the con artist promises, echoing our measure
of *true, truth, trust*—the new syllables
solid on our tongues, ready to speak,
speaking.

Begin

Just a single, rough, gray pebble,
as slight as a fingernail,

as tiny as a chip off a full-formed
wish, like an irritant wedged

between foot and sandal that could,
with much patience and persistence,

be saved and made into something
not big but on its way to small

then—eventually—larger: a statue, even,
holding up a torch. But this is not

about construction. There are a zillion
crushed stones as far as your peripheral

vision can see. And they are monochrome
and crowded. And they are as tall as twin towers

and wrap around the world. Face the wall.
Put your hands on it, your fingers a chisel.

It is a single, rough, gray pebble.
Start with that.

II

What Still Breathes

In the Company of Women

Always, they are surprised
by the boulder-sized heft of the hidden
beneath the weight of my ordinary eyes
that smoke-signal they, too, will survive
give or take a decade or two; give or take
the unrelenting midnight whys
that unwind into others' lives,
the discovery of lifting,
rock by rock, pebble by pebble,
what once was thrown as "Victim!"
but, now, weight-lifted together,
becomes stone bridge, becomes
path home.

Found and Not Found

And when I lost you on the beach,
you were crossing only the threshold of the tide—

the Atlantic, not the Suchiate River or the Gulf—
and when discovered ten long moments later,

you raised your small hand and waved,
unaware of the terror in a parent's empty arms.

Go back, young one, to the life you never lost
to find those crying for the hand

that held them all night across the rough
crossing, only to lose them now in the dead

of night beside a border where patrols,
working the late shifts, grieve for their own

screaming children, much farther away
than the arm's length these small ones know

no longer. Lost child of mine
who grew up to flee far beyond

the search for sand dollars and shells,
hover over these unprotected strangers,

as tiny as you were
when the great ocean roared

its omens and you turned
quickly back into my seeking arms

aware only that someone
larger than you had desperately

called your name. Go now.
Do the same.

To Conjugate

And this is what it's like when the dead still
sleep in your house, fill up their travel coffee mugs,
then sail off in their spray-painted clunker cars
to haunt your house long-distance, absence
thicker than the moldy crusts of pizza
stashed under their bed, than the condoms
still tight in their square packages
stuck in boxes of discarded tea;
than the three-month layers of calls
stacked unanswered on your low-
battery phone. You have been

here before, but what has that
to do with wisdom or the howl
gnawing in your belly
where the dead once grew? Alive
and not, eventually you'll join
the stench of the discarded
stapled to the air; become
the wail that hovers in every room,
stretches towards the locked window,
the one that no longer is, unable
now to swing wide

to broken horizons and the view
of what still breathes
without even the past
tense of you.

Motorcycle Ride

The curve she didn't curve around
straightens her life into rows
of cornfields she'll zoom through
in dreams that turn
into months of coma,
into a cracked skull and lacerated eye
that still sees in that foggy mist of morning
the speed that frees us from everyday
asphalt, just another rule to follow,
all lines the same.

Even here,
in this new day's dim light,
she'd fling her helmet to the horizon,
rev up and fly into forever,
if only she could move her
two eyelids, the thin limbs
silent at the hip. If
only the unending
jagged lines on this boxed-in
screen would straighten. Listen
closely to hear her
leaving.

Story Retold as Half Triolet

On Mother's Day, she jumps out of the car.
The traffic swerves and brakes. Nobody dies.
This is the broken family that they are
on Mother's Day. She jumps. Out of the car,
she runs away. The highway is the scar
they can't escape, the *if* they hear her cry
to Mother. That day, she jumps. Outside the car,
traffic swerves. She breaks nobody. Survives.
This is the frightened family that they are
the Mother's Day she jumps out of the car
and runs. The way is high and hard, the scar
can't be escaped, no *if* about her cry
of "Mother!" Today, she runs. They jump out of the car
to brake the pain. Their bodies' traffic swerves.
                                    Will they survive?

Prodigal Bipolar

Rebellion's a ribbon to wear in her bright, black hair
while she dances the jig with the neighbor's squealing pigs
and three convict sons. No one ever shakes a head and says,
"Girls will be girls." Not one. Not to the fretting parents who wring
their own necks in worry, who sing their own dirge to the sound
of strokes and stress. Not to the twirling deserter. Sex, the great
distinguisher, the great bearer of expectations, the great deceiver of grief
also confesses, "A child will be a child," but even here finds no relief
in equality, the agreed-upon diagnoses trampled in the mud
of some faraway farm while they wait, bruised ears to the ground,
for resounding footsteps that do not come, and do not come again,
the oxen rotted on the spit, the spoiled and rancid stinking up their now-
mortgaged estate in its own slaughtered, gender-neutral, bloody-bad way.

St. Dymphna

— Patron saint of the mentally ill and victims of incest

After your mum's death,
your father's cracked heart

fractured further his broken
cerebrum. It's then he claimed

you as substitute wife *after, after, after . . .*
in his grief, his large Irish hands grabbing

what wasn't his. And you fled
after, after, after, after

across the water, the sands, beyond
the hills to Belgium, where that same

papa who loved your mama, yes, him,
in his deep derangement, raised the arm

that loved the one you both loved—
kind woman who bore you—

and with his tensed muscles
struck down the priest-friend

who came along to guard you and
*after, after, after . . .*this daddy, this

husband to your mommy, sliced
the pure skin of your neck

until your prayers owned no mouth
to come from. O headless heroine,

bathed in the blood of your own horror,
and ours, and the obsessed mourning

of a man cut clean from reason,
where will this *after, after, after* take us?

Where shall we hide from the pain that bore us,
from the damaged selves that keep us dying?

Details

The age? Sometime before
grown, before scream, before
bedtime story, before this is how
you were born. *The person?*
Does it matter? *The hand?*
The right one. *The room?* Dark
and darkening and sometimes
the spark of a face looking elsewhere
in time or place but not thinking
of who or for how long
or for ever after her life. *And where
were the others?* That information is
unavailable. *And why did he put her hand
there?* That information is unavailable.
It was dark and it hurt. This is
how your parents make babies. This is
how the nightlight left on when everyone else
is gone reminds her to spot-clean the sheet,
tuck the moist fabric around her innocence.
And how often? That information is unavailable.
Shut your eyes, she thinks. Pretend to fall,
she remembers, faster and faster asleep.
Will it stop? she wonders. *My,
how you've grown, are growing,*
says the close stranger strangely.
She does not remember his voice,
but it is soft. *Good,*
she thinks it said once. *Good-
night.* She does not remember
her answer. She does not remember
if she answered at all.

Sensory

— *after "the incident"*

What it smells like
she can't remember, but not
like dirt or dust or cum,
not like backwoods or back doors
or back yards. Back when she could
remember, it didn't smell. Smell
didn't hang low or often. Often,
she's told, sniff is the portal
to memory but why portal the whiff
of this? Back when she had nostrils
that inhaled the whiff of who and when,
she had taste buds. Taste she remembers.

#MeToo

Today our words stick in the click of keys,
reshape their sounds. It's hard to mourn a past
you've thrown away without an elegy
to mark its pain. And yet all grief outlasts

the syllables we grab to make a poem
that looks like us. This permanence we share
is what we write, the scars and tongue our own.
The secret letters link our *here* and *there*,

inscribe a life caught tight between the lines
and lies of someone's louder voice, and yet
the narrative will out. The past, both mine
and yours, will tell its days of deep duress

and live to type another self: We claim
one life rewrites the rest. But they're the same.

Pact

"The deaths of two Saudi sisters . . .
discovered on the banks of New York's Hudson River . . .
a double suicide." CNN, 10/29/18

Together. Our thin-
lipped secrets protecting
the dead and the living, the ones who did not
protect us, never will. We have measured and cut
the rope, tied it around our bared necks. Pulled the strands taut.
There is no truth in the telling, no telling in the truth that tightens
into this noose. Will you dangle here with me?
I with you?
           This is the sisterhood we dreamed
           and feared,
      but, wait,
               over there is

the small jutting pier at Riverside Park, and there the two
Saudi Arabian sisters. See. They are duct-taped together
at ankles and wrists. They have not
been long in the water. No one
suspects foul play. Look
how their dark curls
float about them.
           There is time Is there
time? There is.
            Let us cut our own
Is there time? There is   despair
    Is there?
        and save them. Here is

Is there?   the knife.
                Do it now.

Q & A: Two Friends, One Week

—for S. L. and S. M., during the California fires
in November 2018

I.
Leave home/return home
to the already-burning
real fire of forests near sands,
to the fanned anger of a man
aflame with the pain of combustion
hurled at others, at you? *Leave.* Heat rises
quickly to the neck, bruises tightening.
"The air," friends warn, "is heavy with ash
and fear." Even before the news flashes "Danger!"
his presence sears. Take nothing
but your breath. Flee the embers
of what was but is
no more. Burn every key.

II.
Leave home/stay home
from the pretend last-ditch ultimatum
he insists you owe him, fantasy the trap
he keeps setting? *Stay.* A good man can still snap
in the snare of claiming the coveted (which is
you, which is always you), the expected
the trigger he's timed his life by.
Even the well-meaning can, in the flash
of the unforeseen—anger or rejection—ignite
the chain reaction, *bitter* exploding
into *entitled* into *revenge*, the pungent
smoke of warning rising
too late, too late.

Night Train

No matter the neighborhood,
you find me, your rough song of clacks
inches above the bed I've hauled
from trailer to condo to suburb
where all my dreams remain the same
hobo-style hopping into your wide-open
rusted cars that hum and thump past the horizon
into a country not here. Listen
to the way your voice calls me at 3:00 a.m.
to read your faraway moving graffiti,
to memorize your landscapes of what is passing by.
But now I am dreaming of who I am here
in this neighborhood that are just tracks to you,
tracks, and more tracks,
a blur that, finally, never answers
such urgent whistles, *Wake! Rise! Go!*

Cortisol: This Is Only a Test

that measures the thickness of bricks,
the density of cinder,
the weight of nails,
the length of boards,
the height of forever,
the depth of never,
the circumference of always that measures
the way you remember
or don't, the panic, the pressure,
the pain, the mixture
of mortar and memory
that blocks the synapse,
the names, the street, the day, the why
of what was said, the when,
the details drenched in stress,
the hormones hammered, the constant
construction of cortisol,
stone by stone for weeks,
for months, for years, for decades.
This is the brain that was built,
worry by worry, crisis by crisis,
everything not tumbling down
but up into this lonesome, loathsome
wailing wall that only the brave can chip,
tip, knock, dismantle, bombard, blast, decimate,
eradicate, obliterate, annihilate. Now.
Remember?

Ode to "Normal"

Between crises,
Normal enters as faint memory,

mannerisms we knew once-upon-a-time,
now fresh from the shower, blonde hair dripping,

long legs hop-clicking two steps at a time down
the front stairs just in time for flank steak

and garlic mashed potatoes, which Normal
passes ever so politely to the right.

How to high-five the return of the missing,
prostrate ourselves before the stranger

unexpectedly resurrected from pain
in time for an ordinary Saturday?

We swallow our songs of praise,
sit on hands anxious to applaud,

refuse the almost unbearable urge
to breakdance on the kitchen table.

"Here," we say to Normal, "is the un-
fatted calf cooked to your liking, and over here

is your favorite childhood dessert. So good
to have you. Please come again."

Ode to Exhaustion

Deep down in the bones,
below stretched muscle

and mind that can't contain
another ounce of the world's

work or worry, the body gives up
its sense of sinews and soul,

gives in to last-ditch denial
of sleep where something beyond

waking boundaries of burnout
and the broken and weary-worn evaporates

into almost-forgotten levitation: you hovering
in another realm not here, depleted, restored.

Poetic Psychoanalysis: Graceland

All week, the entire town in sequins—
pompadoured teens,
side-burned street vendors,
pant-suited septuagenarians—
their foreheads and chests slick with sweat,
their hips gyrating in sequence, yet—
more surprisingly—in this poem, it's my first-time-to-Memphis trek,
and somehow I've slipped through the thick-as-grits crowd
and am giddily maneuvering my suddenly svelte self
up flower-strewn stairs of the King's mansion
past the secret-service types guarding the master suite
and into the padlocked bathroom of pure mystery
of what happened when and how and why
it should matter to you, the reader,
who are dreaming your own poetic investigation
beyond the barricaded second-floor doors of Graceland
or wide-open windows of grace that,
yes, leave us grateful *and* greedy,
wanting one more wailing hymn
or crooning ballad. We've all paid
the entrance fee.

Postmenopausal Blues

No, not Blues, more of a tango with the self.
No, not dusty Blues, I'm talkin' a tango with the self,
purple scarves flowin' 'round my sexy shelf
of a bosom as I leave those bummer Blues
all by themselves somewhere else.

No, not tango, but a ballet with the self.
No, not sultry tango, I'm talkin' ballet by myself.
Wispy, sequined tulle, swirling the svelte
inside figure of myself, yeah, the body that I've felt
pirouetting into sixty, dancing by myself.

No, not ballet, but break-dancing by myself.
No, not graceful ballet; I'm talking raucous, rowdy self
celebrating decades, letting loose my woman's wealth
of wisdom till I spin around with sisters. Lonely Blues?
No, not singin' Blues. Singin' sisters. Singin' self.

Hyphen

And in the on-line photo you Googled in a split-
       second of nostalgia before re-
filling your cup of cold coffee in the middle of grading half-
       assed and in-
accurate freshman essays about love, your ex-
       lover, once so gallant and handsome in his pre-
abuse days, now poses half-
       in/half-
out of the framed, somewhat professional-
       looking ad for brain-
health, and he is (can it be, the one-who-finally-stopped-barging-
       into-your-dreams with his semi-
cocked, alluring grin; yes, him) is huge—as in bigger-
       than-the-cave-he-carved-beneath-your-
ribs huge—and you can't quite recognize his just-
       opened eyes that saw you for you in those before-
dawn moments when you curled slimly into him with no hyphens
       to link you together, no selfies, no Google, no on-
line evidence that this "love" even your oldest students try-try-
       fail to define defines you or raises its hand to pretend-
describe the nameable part of your-
       self that is now, thirty years later, new names with-
out hyphens, without definitions, with-
       out, without.

And yet—
       you are happy to be not-
happy or at least not un-
       happy to be surprised somewhat-
happy at this not-quite-but-almost-
       turn into memory, into the strange world of then-
and-now, with now better after-
       all, at least today when your un-
tanned, pale suburban leg falls asleep as you are slow-
       typing this, but is finally fast-waking

into a morning where it is time for more fresh-
      ground, bitter-
sweet coffee that you can, with now-
      awake limbs, amble to the re-
modeled kitchen and refill the chipped cup as your not-
      new love looks up from the paper, rises in his most-
      ordinary of ways, and smiles—
just like that—no dash, not even half
      a hyphen in his eyes
as he offers to warm what you have.

Ode to Husband as Fanatic

          Praise
for the whole-
hearted and die-
hard, nit-picky
in passion, particular
in palm-waving for—
not music, but the ride 'em high
and low of jazz;
          not baseball,
but the drive 'em long and far
and give up the field
for the Fenway Faithful;
          not grilling,
but the turn 'em, the sauté
and never burn 'em—
steak and onions in heat wave;
shish-kabobs in blizzards;
asparagus wrapped tightly
in fresh during unexpected
April s eet.
          And praise
for semi-secret societies
and secret-concoction salmon;
for the sacred and oft-venerated
grill covers, sweatshirts, coats,
mittens, blankets, pillows, light
switches, lamps, flags, signs,
ornaments, jewelry, keyboards, flash
drives, coffee cups, salt shakers,
shoelaces, socks of Red Sox
and Weber logos welcoming
each sunrise w th aficionado
and bravo!

And, all hail
the well-lighted photo shoot
of Thanksgiving turkey,
Christmas prime rib;
the smoky sanctity of beans,
but also the daily devotion to god-
forsaken grammar, to teaching,
to sound and sense and the recipe
of story served up as appetizer
or sit-down full course
as preparation for conversation:
baseball, grilling, God—
all serenaded by Thelonious.
O sing loud
the layered song of sentences
entwining tale and taste,
the last play and Last Supper,
smoky incense swirling up
towards the patron saint
of selective loyalty: you
who savor liturgy over
spontaneous prayer;
missal rhythms over
Xeroxed praise song,
your chant (acceptable
substitute for Coltrane)
always Gregorian.
So glory be
to God and hot coals,
to home runs, to late-night
jams, to Holy Days, to you
of the fierce beliefs,
who loves not every
song, team, grill,
ritual, person, just
one, just fan-of-you,
just me.

Ode to Memory

O, you, in your slinky slip of late middle age,
turning the corner down a long dark hall
at the end of forever ago, fuzzy in the dusky light—
so say the movies, even the black-and-whites
crackling at twilight behind my eyes
or the whispered shadowy sightings
of *The Shining* dancing the past away
scenes before Jack Nicholson axes through
the present-moment bathroom door
to Shelley Duvall, "Here's Johnny,"
our most memorable hauntings—
each with its own maniacal grin—
calling out, swinging the sharp object.

But this is an ode, not thriller,
and, dear Memory, here you pull close
with comfort, raise high the African Violet
and the half-smile of a child I met once at Walmart;
here you rejoice in the regal angles of the Adirondacks
that morning I woke to sunrise and retreating bear.

O Hail your vivid coat of dazzling colors
worn with pride in southern sky and driveway oil spill.
Praise be the albino squirrel struggling with apple core
that first day of fall, 1982, no reasoning, Memory,
in what you covet or cast off, discard on a whim,
or pull in to your overly sentimental heart
and its aged chambers—no logic, except,
perhaps, this: texture of unshaven cheeks,
aroma of soap and skin lingering decades,
you, Memory, wearing me;
future-tense me still clothed
every inch in you and him.

Arise

—July, 2018, during the Thailand cave rescue

This is the prayer of all parents
in whispers, in screams, in the near-silent
gasp sinking to groan outside the dark cave
of the dead and the maybe-gone (who can tell
what the gruesome air is chewing), the unknown
hovering its blind hope too high,

too high. This is your language; this
mine, lament swirling the undercurrent
of belly, twisting the tunnels' neck
into blind holes, dead ends,
while the now-maimed but still
living parents beg, "Arise, come forth!"

"Come forth!" the doctor-priest I don't know
commands my child, who has barricaded
herself behind boulders of her own making—
too large. "Too large," she cries when the divers
swim under, around; instruct her to breathe
more deeply the length of her labyrinth

that turns now into stones not thrown
but shouldered by the belief of swimmers,
by the petitions of ancients, by the precise
calculations of strangers marking the thin space
between supplications rising daily
in a common language of grief

or relief swallowed again and again in the narrow
cavern of waiting, someone else's words
bobbing steadily in the dark night of the cold,
the faithful ritual of rescue ready to begin
again for this child, and this one, and even
mine, miles below belief and barely breathing.

III

Holding Close Each Breaking Day

Self-Portrait after Memory

After as in *submerged*,
as in cut-of-nowhere wave
of vision whooshing back the past
she thought she'd drowned from.

And *after* as in *rising up*,
the wet's crescendo, the bright
rays across sand S.O.S.-ing a story
she knew she knew, keeps knowing.

And there were dangers
and sun, and someone screaming
for popsicles, and the gulls swooping
her full name: first and last.

And *after* becomes *tense*,
as in *is*, as in *continuing to be*
in this ever after of now, for now,
where she recognizes your own

aging hand held out to her
like this, and she takes it,
begins in her steady voice
to tell her story of *after*.

Alzheimer's Aubade

She wakes to gray. No words to guide the way
towards son. His unfamiliar face seems kind
enough. She nods hello. Just yesterday
she knew his eyes, but now? This morning's mind

welcomes the past but not the day. She was
someone: woman who woke at 3:00 a.m. to sing
her restless son to sleep, his calm her cause
for celebration. Today the dawn brings

no clarity, yet still the stranger comes
and draws her curtains wide. She thinks outside
is where she left her life: daughters, a son
who meet sunrise without her. Look, the light

is brighter now. The kind man helps her stand.
To see the morning sun, she takes his hand.

Memory's self-portrait

is, she claims, photographic,
with just the right light (streaming
from a shoulder-high window)
and angle (wide, please). Still,
she insists on the still shot—
nothing in process of becoming,
video verboten—and her stylish right
to choose appropriate aperture of outfit,
time, and—when forced outside
her inside comfort zone—weather.
Too sunny or foggy and she's not her-
self, or yours—just some babe
glitzed up for the shoot. If possible,
keep in sight the total picture—
when posed perfectly, she forgets
to remember that bright-clad tourist
just outside her vision: you
clicking away so quickly.

The Billboard

"It's your word against our video,"
the billboard keeps flashing
as we rush past late one afternoon
on one of those highways that goes on forever
but not into *ad nauseam*, because true is still true
we want to believe, traveling circuitously
cross-country 100 miles an hour in our rented goodwill
with the hood down and our unbleached hair flying out behind us,
past the White House and Pittsburgh; past Dallas and *House of Cards*;
past Oz, *West World*, Hollywood; past childhood's *Twilight Zone*;
past prairie dogs popping like clockwork in and out of holes
dug all the way to China; past KGB pre-programed tumbleweeds
wire-tapping wind; past all these and back to the free
wild world of the badlands. Sure, you can ride with us.
It's a constitutionally alternative-options earth. Catch up. We're not
slowing down. Jump in.

The List

— November 7, 2018; Thousand Oaks, CA

After the search of names—last, first—
attached to the dead, the dying, the "only"
wounded, the always scarred, we fear

in our mouths, the sounds articulated,
the nicknames donned by mothers,
fathers, siblings, friends before

the killer became the killer,
before—or while—the becoming
already began in a word or a glance,

in a name called without thinking,
a syllable stressed unnecessarily,
the bad joke tossed off as jest,

by someone we know, or don't know
well, or met in passing, fear in that
everyday uncomfortable undercurrent

of conversation off just enough
to make us look twice and then again
over our already burdened shoulders

into the face of him or her or you or me
or my student who, twenty years ago,
crept, while I slept at 3:00 a.m.,

up to my small house on a hill
to leave in my rusted mailbox
hand-scrawled poems, pages of them,

unattached to any name,
his authorship anonymous until,
semesters later in a class, I recognized

the rage, the rush of wound,
the tight urgency of words,
the half-broken letters in a name

which is half the name of the former
marine who, last night at 11:20 p.m.,
stormed into Borderline Bar & Grill

and murdered someone else's students,
friends, daughters, sons. All morning,
irrationally, I search old emails

for the names—last, first—
and calculate ages, not of the dead,
but of the killers, of the students

gone, I don't know where,
taking with them the pain
they hoarded, or spat at others,

but also their jagged and
transcendent images that named
the wounded and wounding

whose names I try now to speak—
last, first—into this dangerous air,
into this world of constant weeping.

Unholy Days

—Tree of Life Synagogue, Pittsburgh, PA
(October 27, 2018)

And still what has already begun
continues in its beginning each second
the news captions click into place,

three days and yet more horror,
such sinister trinity of rage and now
the Sabbath splattered. Broken,

we come to Sunday, open our palms
beyond such swallowing of sorrow
that now implodes in the throat, shatters

the semblance of words, re-detonates
in the ears and the brain: babies' screams—
a bris, a baptism; the one teen, the many,

the crucifix penetrating; the brothers
bathed in blood on the synagogue floor;
the Mass mangled, a priest cleansing

his hands of cum; the pipe bombs
packed on trucks traversing through
your neighborhood, to your doorstep, to mine.

What else tied up, packaged, stamped
with a seal of allowance in this country
of kneeling and rising where recited prayers

mark a target on the faithful from inside walls
and out, and children elect the risk
of attendance, obedience and rebellion

both ammunition for someone who wants
you/me gone. O God of suffering,
O deserted, murdered God,

wounded and weeping,
we lay our temples of blood
at your twisted feet.

The Four Horsepersons of the Apocalypse

camp at the edge of forever,
dawn a promise they've stopped

keeping. Multiplication
is the hymn they've memorized

early. Their wa‑ cry of spears
and bows rattle

their raddled brains.
It is easier to copulate

themselves into clones,
dispatch the youngest—bloody

from birth—into the prayerful
plagues of bang and whimper,

into the blazing
disease of obedience,

trot, trot, little horse,
trot, trot.

Hide

here, underground, from the bright
lies of your hope, from the dark
lure of their help, from the bold
thirst of their call

hunker down. this recycled breath
burns, but gulp it anyway. you've
stocked well the metal shelves,
brought decks of cards. solitary
isn't lonely when you win

shuffle. deal. ace, king, queen
transform eventually to tarot.
you can play that, too, waiting
for the Fool, grand conversationalist

that he is, chewing the fat
of your existence, blah-blah-
blahing about his dawn after
the storm, those little white words
that keep ticking in your generator-
powered brain of a clock

hidden somewhere before
you were hidden in this home
below and outside the horror
of not waking to a kiss,
the coffee, a working radio
still playing oldies.

What Her Teacher Said about Nagasaki and Hiroshima

—for d'Ann

She said what
she said was "If you look *she said was*
straight up into the horror of
was she said not sun
she said but bomb *was what she said* exploding suns,
exploding *decimating what she said was* us
she said what she said and your eyes *ours*
hers theirs what she said was
melting, melted would melt." And that is
                                    everything is all
she *was what she* said *was*
is was *what* she *said* That is all
she remembers
she.

Blues, now,

even in the brain, in the rests
broken with the pain
of not knowing your own
notes, your own voice.
It's a cruel stranger
that encores the dementia dirge
and tricks even the soul-
ful into forgetting the name-
sake.

O, Fats, O, Etta—
Ain't That a Shame and
Fool That I Am got switched at the synapse
and all that jumbles the soul
clogged up and stopped singing
the self. Still,

mellow Fats, when those cats
sang you gone with Katrina,
you knew to insist that
behind those silent lips, you're still
blues-ing and twisting.

And, Sassy Etta,
when last winter caught you
rolling death, tell me you remembered,
somewhere in your blues-infused brain
to cat-call all of us,
then belt out *At Last* again.

Tip

of the tongue
not tickling the undiscovered decay;
of the finger, stubbed into silence;
of the #2 pencil, poised and pointed,
suddenly stifled, its nonpoisonous lead
unable to undo any *tabula rasa*—mine or yours
or my mother's, who keeps asking with the tongue
and the finger and the blank slate
of her almost ninety-year-old face,
"How old? How old?"

How old this silence that faces
the poised, the stubbed mother tongue—
yours, mine—blank as any *tabula rasa*
before words knew how to rise,
or fingers how to point at the poisonous,
the decayed, or merely the undiscovered
hiding behind the stifled face,
ninety #2 pencils unable to answer
such sudden questions.

How to answer what tickles the stubbed mind,
undo the poisonous—yours, mine—
face the *tabula rasa* without pencil or tongue,
the blank of silence its own discovery of decay,
the pointed "How old? How old?" suddenly stifled,
leading back to the undoing: blank slate
where ninety keeps asking after itself
as the finger points in question, and the poised
tongue raises again its unanswered

Tip

That Sound

Respirations soaked in saliva,
now pooling up between throat, airway;
here, beyond; the rattle of hospice
and hospital; of farewell coating
muscle and cartilage, a larynx
that articulates loss and love
in bodies we don't want to leave
yet, the way your father's clatter,
slowed and waited as you climbed
the nursing home's stairs two at a time
to see his eyes focus (we tell ourselves)
on you, his only child, both your and his breath
steady, almost sound-less, before death's commotion
forced his lungs' deepest groan out
and into that other room of grief
we knew we'd walk in.
                         Or how,
betrayed by my commitment
to this world's obligations, I arrived
too late to hear my father's noisy exit
a state away, his delayed but rattling ride
to that other state of being not waiting
for my good intentions. "It's for the best,"
my sister said, but even now regret wells up
in the trachea, swells the tongue,
chokes all the words I meant to say
or did when we forgave each other.
                  Or how
                         and not how
that stranger on YouTube recorded
on her phone someone she loved, someone
named Ron whose rattling keeps her re-playing
the loss she breathes in and out, the heaving
still the signifier of happiness lost
and—not replaced—but something
close to respiration eventually
filling up the lungs of the daily.
                Like that and not

when I sat two days with your father,
surrogate for mine, holding hands,
singing the old hymns of heart, lungs, throat
and what we held there daily of him,
and would continue to replay as litany
without regret or death-bed recordings
now and now
            and now again.

The pretty aide at the nursing home,

you tell us, doesn't remember her own name,
forgets she used to work in another town

two hours away at Hiester Lanes
where, for thirty years, you bowled near-perfect games

in that other life where you walked and drove
and lived sometime long before now in this unfamiliar town

near us, where she insists she's always lived.
Daily, she smiles, shakes her head, claims she's never held

a bowling ball, cheered loudly for your league
or any other, never learned to keep score.

Still, after trimming your toenails,
rubbing lotion on your cracked skin,

adjusting the TV to *American Bowling Congress,*
and re-filling your empty paper cup, she's remembered

to sneak in an extra sugar cookie, leftover
from yesterday's Valentine's Day party

from which she wheeled you back to your room
early when you began to weep for what she refuses,

even now, to recall of a life she did not have,
in a town she's never seen,

at a place she did not work, using the name
that you insist she declines, even now, to remember.

Self-Portrait as Memory

Her eyes blur with what once was,
gray matter tinted with doubt.

She remembers her skin
before her face was lifted

and the cheek her son kissed
as a toddler in the morning light,

but this rearrangement by age
and scalpel claims a scenario

skewed, old photos just off center
of today's snap-click, her daughter's

nose not quite hers anymore—
and the stories she hears,

settling in ears that first knew a few
centimeters of shift when the slack

of neck was stretched up and over—
even this alters the telling

of the yet unfo ding, reframes
the refractions of light as she leaves daily

her down-sized apartment
through its unbreakable glass door,

which now shimmers her familiar
reflection alongside such new

strange questions: Is this
the face her children remember

when remembering *before*?
Or is it the other?

Manners

Always a lady, she compliments
the hospital bed and its ups and downs,
the gray-mashed beans, the flavorless broth,
and me, who knows "so very much" about
myself, "an excellent researcher" to have discovered
her writer daughter, who also, coincidentally,
is named my name, which she's always loved.
Don't I love it, too?

"Such a small world," she murmurs
before asking me to please
pass the No-Salt salt.

She shivers. I help her tug
the thin cover up evenly to her chin.
When my sister returns to the room
with a newly warmed blanket
and the nurse she has gone to fetch,
then sits with me again at the bedrail,
my polite mother asks, "Have you met
my other daughter? The beautiful one?"
"Yes," I nod. "She's lovely."

When her mind and body
again thrash violently
and "for her own protection" (the aides explain)
they strap her into a straightjacket,
my mother pleads with us to find
her daughters, who "are always happy to help."
"Thank you so much," she smiles,
before glaring at us suddenly
with someone else's impolite eyes.

Always a lady, my mother
does not know that she's not
who she is at the moment
swearing at the nurses she thinks
are strangling her, at the intern
who, surely, has stolen her car,
the one we will take away
"for her own protection,"
after the MRI and CT Scan,
after the final diagnosis: common
infection that hijacked her brain

temporarily, which she will not remember
when she returns to her polite small talk,
to the well-mannered children she recognizes
and calls by name, the names she's always loved.
Don't we love them, too?

Self-Portrait with Memory

Always, it seems, she is a younger *she*,
standing too close to your creaking
shoulders and bad knees, too close
to your almost-deaf ear where she talks
too loudly for too long about people and places
you can't remember from far away; too close
to the crows-feet around your eyes; too close
to red-veined spiders trekking across thighs,
to age spots multiplying on the backs of hands
that try to swat her away, then—suddenly—for the love
of Memory, draw her too close—or not close enough—right here
beside your forgetful heart, beside all your automated
rhythms of open, close; open, close.

My Mother Sends Birthday Cards

This year, she remembers
everyone—daughter, daughter-in-law,
son-in-law, grandchildren—but early,
March Hallmarks arriving before
September's almost-autumn,
age a wish we'd rather wait on
but still welcome with open mail slots
when her stamped blessings
arrive cross-country,
annotated and pre-season.

Again, she has forgotten
herself: her ninetieth
one day before my real,
new-decade celebration
still six months in the future.
I keep her card, but save
for our October ritual
of burning leaves,
the useless calendar.

In the changing air,
from now until spring,
or too-early, unseasonable death,
I'll toast her daily, postmark
card after card after card
after card with no space
whatsoever for any
return address.

Exhibit: Memory Loss

—a series by artist Judi Kirsch (Takoma Park, Maryland)

Beige,
      variations of grays, black—

the artist's twines of logic uncurl,
      re-coil eccentrically
         over ill-defined mass
   of dark confusion, thin rope-like
neuron-like
      fiber-like (what happened
to my world-like?)

      untied-up ends
overlapping and
interlacing each
   half-loop

     loosened and tightened
       seconds
       days
       decades only to un-
ravel again
   again.   See.

The end is not
in sight. Mother,
come look.

Dusk

The way the clouds hang low, it could be noon
or late fall; she doesn't know the season
or the time. In her mind, the days make room
for meals, for bathroom trips. No reason

to remember where, why. She knows someone
will arrive to take her there, will prepare
the necessary plans, will know the when
of her leaving, the coat she'll need to wear

to brace herself from cold. Perhaps it's snow
that filters out the light. Perhaps it's dusk,
the long chill drawing close. And yet, she hopes
it's spring, late day, the world's worries hushed

as she slips now towards sleep. Always the gray
darkens to night. She does not know the day.

A few moments after a fall at her assisted living facility, my mother forgets

the tepid shower, how her body tipped
backwards off the stool, over the tub,
head smacking bathroom tile. The surprised aide
reaches too late the frail body, tries to rewind time:

the fallen body back in the tub, on the stool.
The second before, the aide is soaping the thin torso;
the second after, she is reaching too late the frail body
sprawled on the cold floor. The daughter comes running.

The second before, the aide soaps the thin torso,
turns to adjust the spray, then the clatter,
the naked woman sprawled on the cold floor. The daughter running
in from the other room, afraid. Whose face is screaming?

Turning to adjust the shower's spray, the aide hears the clatter.
Her hands slippery, she cannot catch the woman
or, afraid, face the one from the other room. Every face is screaming.
Is there blood? Is she breathing? Lift and cradle her.

Her hands slippery, she cannot catch the woman
whose every bone protrudes. Will they break?
Is there blood? Is she breathing? Lift and cradle her.
She is as light as a corpse.

Her every bone protrudes. Did they break?
"Old woman, hold me tight, smile at your daughter.
You are as light as a corpse
but yourself, alive enough to forget

everything." The old woman smiles at the daughter, holds tight the aide
who carries her to safety, dries her, puts her to bed.
Alive, she is enough herself
to forget everything. After the fall, she is

dried, carried safely to bed. The rest fades:
no head smacking the tile, no surprised aide.
She is herself, alive, a daughter beside her. It is enough.
No tepid shower (her body tipping),

no cold tile, no surprised aide.
Safe in bed, the rest fades.
Tepid memories tip. After the fall, she forgets.
She is alive again only in the moment. Is it enough?

I Watched You Disappear

—for Anya Krogovoy Silver

or didn't because—on watch
these two, fifteen, forty years

for father, friends, me, you—
death still sneaks up and around

the already grieving, still
circles back in broad daylight, interrupts

bland conversations of let's meet here
and when, then stuffs its filthy sock

inside shocked, lipsticked mouths,
halfway down throats

that keep gurgling hope,
keep spouting dates to a calendar

not-blank with Maybe plans. I watched you
not disappear when I was not

here nor there, on-time or late;
not hovering in the half-light of emergency,

the gray Rorschach of X-rays,
or the stiff uncertainty of chairs

lined up by un-sterilized bedsides
where I did not hold in my damaged heart

his final breath, her glassy stare,
their wispy half-spoken words

that mix with yours
in the broken laughter of your last

typed joke, which I didn't see
until now when you reappeared—

just like that—on the stark screen
of this saved page,

your resurrected humor blooming
again and again and again.

Still Life with Rabbits and Phone

It is only a rabbit hunkered down
in this fenced-in backyard
two thousand miles from her,
91 and frail, inside the locked
Assisted Living apartment,
not here.

Each day, across invisible sound waves,
my mother and I name and re-name the hare,
the bunny, the cottontail, the lapin,
the breathing bundle of fur and ears
hopping in and out of our words,
memories, what we string across miles
and years.

And I have fallen in love with the rabbit
who returns each evening to a small patch
of dying grass in the middle of Central Pennsylvania
while my ailing mother in Arizona
suggests as names "Peter" or "Hoppy" or "Hope."

It is only a rabbit, but one morning—
when my husband and son find it
dragged and gnawed, its insides
exposed to the bloody-black world—
my mouth goes dry, no way to shape
the absence: hare, bunny, cottontail, lapin,
nonbreathing bundle of fur and ears.

Like this, time hops backwards and forwards.
Hours sprawl in the dead grass.
My mother forgets the hare, bunny, cottontail, lapin;
doesn't recall the namings, the conversations.
"Are you sure," she whispers over the phone,
"are you sure I'm in Phoenix? Are you
certain it was a rabbit?"

When I next spy a small gray rabbit
stretched out near the fence,
I dial her number,
exclaim, "What shall we call him? What?"
"Hare, bunny, cottontail, lapin," she lists.
Then, just like that,
she lands again on "Hope."

Ode to Everything

Enough of the lamentations.
       Open the window and sing!
       The world is awash with
world: color-dripping globe always
tilting into some *Ah!* or another,
clouds stretching wide plump happiness,
       even in the noisy stage-show of showers,
       such sunny ovations.
       And the birds—
overpopulating every poem—
swoop here for free—
swallow, hawk, robin, gull, eagle—what else
can be written but wings that wave
horizon to horizon?

And enough of windows.
       Praise doors! Step out
       with arms open, and eyes gathering
       vim and vision: grandeur
trailing from worm and woodchuck,
branch puzzles of woods, open boat of breeze—
all brimming with *Hey!*
       and *Hallelujah!*
       and *Celebrate!* such green giving
of thanks, such miraculous mercy of earth:
calm valley and even this rugged, rocky chain
we climb now as family, claiming praise as respite,
holding close each breaking day, dangerous
       yet divine in all
       its gorgeous glory.

Your Move, Anna Lee Hafer

Acknowledgments

Aethlon: A Journal of Sport Literature and *Aethlon: A Journal of Sport Literature 40th Anniversary Issue,* "Ode to Husband as Fanatic"

America Magazine, "Arise," Winner of the $1000 Foley Poetry Prize

Ars Medica, "This Is Only a Test"

Beautiful Cadaver Poetry Project Pittsburgh, "Postmenopausal Blues"

Bengaluru Review, "Sensory," "Story Retold as Half Triolet," "Unholy Days"

But You Don't Look Sick: The Real Life Adventures of Fibro Bitches, Lupus Warriors, and other Super Heroes Battling Invisible Illness (Indie Blue Publishing Anthology), "After the diagnosis,"

Chautauqua Literary Journal, "Guardian" published as "What She Saw/Sees." "Hide," "Night Train"

Christian Century, "Prodigal Bipolar," copyright © 2019 by the *Christian Century.* Reprinted by permission from the 13 March 2019 issue of the *Christian Century.* christiancentury.org

Christianity and Literature, "Seeing Things"

Cincinnati Review MiCRo section, "Details," 2019 Best of the Net nominee

The Curator, "Motorcycle Ride"

Dove Tales: An International On-line Journal of the Arts, "Begin," "Found and Not Found," "What Her Teacher Said about Nagasaki and Hiroshima"

EcoTheo, "Pact"

The Ekphrastic Review, "Ode to Daughter as Artist"

Frontiers: A Journal of Women Studies, "Hyphen," "In the Company of Women"

The Grotto Network, "Exhibit: Memory Loss," "Ode to Almost-Silence," "Ode to Exhaustion"

Heart Beats (Prolific Pulse Press), "Ode to Almost-Silence"

Hiroshima Day Anthology (Moonstone Press 2022), "What Her Teacher Said about Nagasaki and Hiroshima"

The Innisfree Poetry Journal, "A few moments after a fall at her assisted living facility, my mother forgets"

JAMA, "Alzheimer's Aubade"

Juxtaprose, "On a Hot Summer Night for Revenge"

The MacGuffin, "Q & A: Two Friends, One Week"

Mezzo Cammin, "Dusk"

Misfit Magazine, "The pretty aide at the nursing home"

Mojave River Review, "To Conjugate"

Mom Egg Review, "Suicide Drafts"

Orbis, "Ode to 'Normal,'" "Ode to Son as Encyclopedia"

Pirene's Fountain, "The Billboard"

Plainsongs, "Self-Portrait with Memory"

Plough, "Ode to Everything," "Prayer for Three Women, Twenty-One and Under"

Poetry for the Dementia Journey: An AlzAuthors Anthology, "Dusk," "Self-Portrait after Memory," "Still Life with Rabbits and Phone"

Presence: A Journal of Catholic Poetry, "Photo with Bald Heads"

Relief: A Journal of Art and Faith, "Auto-, Bio-, Graphy"

River and South, "My Mother Sends Birthday Cards"

Southern Florida Poetry Journal, "St. Dymphna," "Tip"

The Southern Quarterly, "Poetic Psychoanalysis: Graceland"

Stone Canoe, "Ode to Memory," "That Sound"

Storms of the Inland Sea: Poems of Alzheimer's and Dementia Caregiving, "Manners," "The pretty aide at the nursing home"

SWWIM, "The artist at the colony asks me if I'm famous," "Self-Portrait as Memory"

Tahoma Literary Review, "#MeToo"

Third Wednesday, "The List"

Through the Looking Glass: Reflecting on Madness and Chaos Within (Indie Blu(e) Publishing Anthology), "Bipolar Triolet," "Guardian" published as "What She Saw/Sees"

Twelve Mile Review, "Self-Portrait after Memory," "Trust,"

Verse Daily, "Self-portrait after Memory," "Trust,"

The Westchester Review, "Still Life with Rabbits and Phone"

Whale Road Review, "The Four Horsepersons of the Apocalypse," "I Watched You Disappear"

When Home Is Not Safe: Writing on Domestic Verbal, Emotional, and Physical Abuse (Exposit Books), "On a Hot Summer Night for Revenge"

Writing in a Woman's Voice (96th Moon Prize), "Ode to Everything," 30 March 2022 and 14 June 2022

In many ways this new collection, Seeing Things, is a prequel to my 2023 book In the *Museum of My Daughter's Mind*, a collaboration with my artist daughter, as well as to my 2022 poetic pilgrimage, *Begin with a Question*. May these poems bring what is most needed—comfort, insight, understanding, empathy, hope—particularly for those who struggle with or care for those with mental and physical disabilities or who have themselves experienced various levels of trauma while searching for truth in a society where the lines of reality often are blurred. Through words and the Word, we find a way through.

I am grateful to the editors of these journals for first publishing these poems, some of which originally appeared under slightly different titles.

The italicized portion of the final stanza of the poem "Seeing Things" is a quotation from Thomas Merton's *Hagia Sophia*.

The title of my poem "I Watched You Disappear" is taken from Anya Krugovoy Silver's 2014 book *I Watched You Disappear* (LSU Press). The poem's last line alludes to her 2017 book *Second Bloom* (Cascade Books).

Many of these poems were written during a wonderfully productive 2013 residency at the Virginia Center for the Creative Arts, for which I received partial funding from Lock Haven University.

I want to offer immense thanks to fellow poets and friends Lois Roma-Deeley, Julie L. Moore, Judith Sornberger, Barbara Crooker, and Gloria Heffernan, for their invaluable encouragement and suggestions, as well as to VCCA comrade Jan Freeman, all of whom emboldened me to navigate difficult subject matter.

I am especially indebted to my daughter, Anna Lee Hafer, for the use of her stunning painting *Your Move*; to designer Melody Standford Martin for the powerful cover; to Ava O'Malley for her creative marketing, and to Wildhouse Poetry Editor Mark Burrows for his perceptive reading and astute advice.

Finally, I have immeasurable gratitude for my husband and our two (now) grown children, Anna Lee and Will, with whom we climbed together "this rugged, rocky chain" to "[hold] close each breaking day."

Professor Emerita of English and Creative Writing at Commonwealth University, **Marjorie Maddox** has published seventeen collections of poetry—including *Transplant, Transport, Transubstantiation* (Yellowglen Prize); *Begin with a Question* (International Book Award and Illumination Book Award); Shanti Arts ekphrastic collaborations *Heart Speaks, Is Spoken For* and *Small Earthly Space* (both with artist Karen Elias), and *In the Museum of My Daughter's Mind* (with her artist daughter Anna Lee Hafer and others). The latter won the 2024 Royal Dragonfly Award for fine art and photography, as well as the 2024 American Fiction Award for poetry. *Hover Here* (Broadstone 2025) is forthcoming. In addition, Maddox has published a story collection and four children's books, has coedited two anthologies, and is assistant editor of *Presence: A Journal of Catholic Poetry*. She hosts *Poetry Moment*, a radio program produced by NPR member station WPSU-FM.

For more information, visit www.marjoriemaddox.com

This book is set in Optima typeface, developed by the German type- designer and calligrapher Hermann Zapf. Its inspiration came during Zapf's first trip to Italy in 1950. While in Florence he visited the cemetery of the Basilica di Santa Croce and was immediately taken by the design of the lettering found on the old tombstones there. He quickly sketched an early draft of the design on a 1000 lire banknote, and after returning to Frankfurt devoted himself to its development. It was first released as Optima by the D. Stempel AG foundry in 1958 and shortly thereafter by Mergenthaler in the United States. Inspired by classical Roman inscriptions and distinguished by its flared terminals, this typeface is prized for its curves and straights which vary minutely in thickness, providing a graceful and clear impression to the eye.